AI OR YOU: FUTURE-PROOF YOUR CAREER IN THE NEXT DECADES

A Strategic Plan for Non-Technicians and Technicians to Succeed in the Age of Artificial Intelligence

By Ivan Kuznietsov

COPYRIGHT AND DISCLAIMERS

Legal Disclaimer:

The views expressed in this book are solely those of the author and do not necessarily reflect the views of any organization the author is affiliated with. The author makes no representations as to the accuracy or completeness of any information provided in this book.

DEDICATION

To all those who embrace the power of AI and strive to shape a future where technology and humanity coexist harmoniously.

EPIGRAPH

"Success is not the key to happiness. Happiness is the key to success. If you love what you are doing, you will be successful." - Albert Schweitzer

ABOUT THE AUTHOR

Hi, my name is Ivan Kuznietsov. I was born in Ukraine and my professional journey has taken me across diverse industries throughout Europe, bestowing me with invaluable insights and experiences along the way. I am a certified Scrum Master and Agile Coach with a deep passion for the world of artificial intelligence (AI). As an avid learner and practitioner in the field of AI, I combine my expertise in Agile methodologies with my enthusiasm for artificial intelligence, using a storytelling approach to demystify complex concepts and make them accessible to readers of all backgrounds.

ABOUT THE BOOK SERIES

This book is a part of *the "AI from A to Z: Decoding Artificial Intelligence for Non-Technicians and Technicians"* series which is a comprehensive guide that takes you on a step-by-step journey through the world of AI. From the basics to advanced topics, each book in the series unravels the complexities of AI and presents them clearly and concisely. Whether you're new to AI or looking to expand your knowledge, this series is your go-to resource for understanding and leveraging the power of AI.

ABOUT THE BOOK

In a world rapidly transformed by the power of artificial intelligence, the question arises: will you be left behind or will you seize the opportunity to shape your future? "AI or You: Future-Proof Your Career in the Next Decades" is a compelling guide that empowers non-technicians and technicians alike to navigate the AI revolution with confidence. Unveiling a strategic plan tailored for success in the age of AI, this book equips you with the tools and insights to stay relevant, seize new opportunities, and forge a future-proof career. Discover how to harness the potential of AI, unlock your true potential, and embark on an exciting journey of growth and prosperity.

PREFACE

Welcome to the world of AI—a realm where innovation knows no bounds and possibilities are limitless. In this fast-paced era of technological advancements, staying ahead of the curve is crucial. "AI or You: Future-Proof Your Career in the Next Decades" serves as your trusted companion on this transformative journey. Through captivating stories, real-world examples, and practical strategies, I will empower you to embrace the AI revolution with confidence. Whether you're a non-technician curious about AI's potential or a technician seeking to sharpen your skills, this book will equip you with the insights and tools needed to thrive in the age of artificial intelligence. Get ready to unlock new opportunities and shape a future-proof career that sets you apart. Let the adventure begin!

CONTENTS

INTRODUCTION: WELCOME TO THE AI REVOLUTION

"The pace of progress in artificial intelligence (I'm not referring to narrow AI) is incredibly fast. Unless you have direct exposure to groups like Deepmind, you have no idea how fast—it is growing at a pace close to exponential." - Elon Musk

I want to tell you one story. Once upon a time, there was a prevailing sense of uncertainty and fear in the world. It was an era marked by rapid advancements in technology, where the boundaries of what was once thought possible seemed to be constantly expanding. This was the dawn of the AI revolution, a transformative period that brought with it great promises and profound concerns.

In the collective consciousness of society, there

loomed a fear that artificial intelligence would replace human beings, rendering our skills and abilities obsolete. The idea of machines taking over our jobs, our livelihoods, and even our very essence was enough to send shivers down the spine of even the most resilient among us.

But let us step back for a moment and reflect on the nature of fear. Fear, at its core, is a primal instinct designed to protect us from harm. It is a powerful emotion that can cloud our judgment and hinder our progress. And yet, fear can also serve as a catalyst for change, propelling us forward into uncharted territories and pushing us to adapt and evolve.

In the face of the AI revolution, it is only natural for these fears to arise. After all, AI has the potential to revolutionize industries, streamline processes, and transform the way we live and work. The rapid advancements in machine learning, natural language processing, and robotics have given rise to intelligent systems capable of performing tasks that were once exclusively the domain of human expertise.

But let me assure you, dear reader, that the purpose of this book is not to dwell on these fears or succumb to the paralyzing grip of uncertainty. Instead, it is to empower you with the knowledge and understanding necessary to navigate this new era and embrace the opportunities it presents.

The AI revolution is not a tale of human versus machine, but rather a story of human-machine collaboration and synergy. It is a partnership that holds the potential to unlock unprecedented levels of innovation, creativity, and efficiency. The true power lies in our ability to harness the capabilities of AI and merge them with our unique human qualities—our ingenuity, empathy, and adaptability.

Throughout the pages of this book, we will embark on a journey together—one that explores the remarkable advancements in AI, delves into the ethical considerations surrounding its use and guides you in harnessing its potential to shape your future. We will delve into the world of AI-driven industries, discover the tools and technologies that can propel your career forward, and explore the skills of the future that will enable you to thrive in this ever-changing landscape.

But above all, we will recognize that the AI revolution is not a singular event, but an ongoing process—a dynamic and evolving ecosystem that requires continuous learning, adaptation, and growth. It is an invitation to embrace change, to shed the shackles of complacency, and to embark on a journey of lifelong learning and personal development.

In the chapters that follow, we will hear stories of individuals who have embraced the AI revolution, like Lucy, who embarked on a path of self-discovery and future-proofed her career. Through her journey, we will gain insights into the transformative power of embracing change, leveraging AI tools and technologies, exploring AI-driven industries, and building a personal brand that stands out in the AI age.

So, dear reader, I invite you to join me on this extraordinary adventure—an exploration of the AI revolution and the endless possibilities it holds. Together, let us uncover the secrets to thriving in this new era, harnessing the power of AI as our ally, and crafting a future that is both human-centered and technologically empowered.

The path before us is vast and full of potential. Are you ready to embark on this journey of discovery and transformation? Welcome to the AI revolution.

PART I: AI OR YOU

"Success in creating AI would be the biggest event in human history. Unfortunately, it might also be the last, unless we learn how to avoid the risks." - Stephen Hawking

CHAPTER 1: EMBRACING THE AI ERA

Once upon a time, in a world not so different from our own, there was a young professional named Sarah. She had been hearing whispers and rumors about a new era, an era of artificial intelligence (AI) that would reshape the very fabric of society. Some saw it as a threat, a force that would steal jobs and render human skills obsolete. But Sarah had a different perspective. She saw the potential, the opportunity, and the possibilities that AI could bring.

As Sarah delved deeper into the world of AI, she discovered that it wasn't about humans versus machines. Instead, it was about humans and machines collaborating, working hand in hand to achieve greater heights. She realized that the key to success in the AI era was not to resist or fear the technology, but to embrace it with open arms.

In this chapter, we will embark on a journey to understand the essence of the AI era and how you can position yourself to thrive in this new landscape. We will explore the transformative power of AI and its potential impact on industries and job markets. So, fasten your seatbelts and get ready to dive into the world of possibilities.

The Rise of AI: Shaping a New Frontier

Imagine a world where intelligent machines can process vast amounts of data, recognize patterns, and make decisions with incredible speed and accuracy. This is the world we find ourselves in today, as AI technology continues to advance at an unprecedented pace. From self-driving cars to virtual assistants, AI has already started permeating our daily lives.

But what exactly is AI? At its core, AI refers to the ability of machines to mimic or simulate human intelligence. It encompasses a wide range of technologies, including machine learning, natural language processing, computer vision, and robotics. These technologies enable machines to learn from data, understand and generate human language, perceive and interpret visual information, and interact with the physical world.

The Impact of AI on Industries

AI is not limited to a single industry. Its influence is far-reaching and can be seen across various sectors. Let's take a look at a few examples to illustrate the breadth of AI's impact.

In healthcare, AI is revolutionizing diagnostics and treatment. Intelligent algorithms can analyze medical images, detect anomalies, and assist doctors in making accurate diagnoses. AI-powered chatbots can provide personalized healthcare advice and support to patients, improving access to medical information and services.

In finance, AI algorithms are used for fraud detection, risk assessment, and algorithmic trading. These algorithms can process vast amounts of financial data in real time, identifying patterns and anomalies that human analysts might miss. As a result, financial institutions can make more informed decisions and minimize risks.

In manufacturing, AI-powered robots are transforming production lines. They can perform complex tasks with precision, speed, and efficiency, enhancing productivity and reducing costs. AI algorithms can also optimize supply chain management, forecasting demand, and streamlining logistics.

These examples represent just a fraction of the potential applications of AI across industries. The rise of AI is disrupting traditional business models, creating new opportunities, and redefining the way we work.

Adapting to the AI Era

Now that we've glimpsed the vast landscape shaped by AI, it's time to explore how you can navigate this new terrain and harness its power for your success.

The first step is to embrace the mindset of collaboration. Remember, AI is not here to replace humans. It is here to augment our capabilities. By embracing AI as a partner rather than a rival, you can unlock a world of possibilities. Think of AI as your powerful ally, working alongside you to enhance your skills, automate mundane tasks, and unleash your creative potential.

Next, it's essential to develop a growth mindset and continuously upgrade your skills. The AI era demands adaptability and a willingness to learn. As new technologies emerge, it's crucial to stay curious, seek out learning opportunities, and acquire the skills that will be in high demand. By nurturing a learning mindset, you can position yourself as a valuable asset in the AI-powered workforce.

Finally, it's important to recognize that the AI era brings with it a changing landscape of work. Some job roles may evolve, while others may become obsolete. This doesn't mean that humans will be left behind. It means that we need to adapt and cultivate uniquely human skills: creativity, empathy, critical thinking, and problem-solving. By embracing these skills, you can carve out a meaningful role in the AI-driven world.

As we conclude this chapter, take a moment to reflect on the opportunities that lie ahead. The AI era is not a threat. It is an invitation to reimagine the way we work, collaborate, and create. By embracing the AI era with open arms, you can future-proof your career and unlock a world of possibilities.

In the next chapter, we will explore how you can unleash your potential in the age of AI and tap into the vast opportunities that await. So, stay tuned, and get ready to embark on an exciting journey of self-discovery and growth.

Remember, the future is AI, and the future is yours to shape!

CHAPTER 2: UNLEASHING YOUR POTENTIAL IN THE AGE OF AI

In a small town nestled amidst towering mountains, there lived a young woman named Maya. Maya had always been fascinated by the possibilities of technology and the ever-evolving world around her. As she watched the rise of artificial intelligence (AI), she couldn't help but wonder how she could tap into its power to unleash her potential.

Maya understood that the age of AI was not a threat to be feared, but an opportunity to be seized. She knew that by embracing AI and harnessing its capabilities, she could unlock new levels of creativity, efficiency, and productivity. With a determined gleam in her eyes, Maya set out on a quest to discover how she could unleash her potential in this exciting new era.

Embracing Lifelong Learning: The Key to Growth

Maya quickly realized that in the age of AI, continuous learning was not just a recommendation but a necessity. The pace of technological advancement was accelerating, and to stay relevant, she needed to be a perpetual student. She adopted a growth mindset, always hungry for knowledge and willing to expand her horizons.

Through online courses, webinars, and workshops, Maya immersed herself in the world of AI. She learned about machine learning algorithms, neural networks, and natural language processing. She discovered how AI was transforming industries like healthcare, finance, and transportation. Maya saw the potential to make a real impact, and her excitement grew.

As Maya dived deeper into her studies, she came across real-world examples of individuals who had unleashed their potential in the age of AI. Take Sarah, for instance, a data scientist who had developed an AI-powered system to predict disease outbreaks. By leveraging her expertise in AI and combining it with her passion for healthcare, Sarah was revolutionizing the field and saving countless lives.

Maya also learned about John, an artist who used AI algorithms to create stunning works of art. By merging his artistic vision with AI tools, John was able to push the boundaries of creativity and produce mesmerizing pieces that captivated audiences worldwide. These stories inspired Maya and showed her the vast possibilities that awaited her.

The Power of Collaboration: Humans and AI as Co-Creators

Maya understood that the true power of AI lay not in replacing humans, but in augmenting their abilities. She realized that collaboration between humans and AI could lead to extraordinary outcomes. Maya's journey to unleash her potential involved working side by side with AI systems, using them as her trusted collaborators.

She discovered that AI could assist her in complex tasks, automate repetitive processes, and uncover insights from massive datasets. For example, she learned about a team of architects who used AI algorithms to generate innovative building designs. By collaborating with AI, they could explore countless design options, optimize energy efficiency, and create structures that blended aesthetics with functionality.

Maya also came across the story of a customer service representative named Alex. With the help of AI-powered chatbots, Alex was able to provide personalized support to customers, resolving their issues more efficiently. The chatbots analyzed vast amounts of customer data, learned from previous interactions, and provided instant solutions. By leveraging AI, Alex was able to elevate the customer experience to new heights.

These examples highlighted the immense potential of humans and AI working together as co-creators. Maya saw the opportunity to apply this collaborative approach in her own field of interest, marketing. She envisioned using AI to analyze customer behavior, predict market trends, and develop targeted marketing campaigns that resonated with audiences on a deep level.

Skills for the AI Era: Cultivating the Human Advantage

Maya understood that to unleash her potential in the age of AI, she needed to cultivate skills that complemented the capabilities of AI systems. While AI excelled at processing vast amounts of data and performing repetitive tasks, it lacked the human touch. Maya recognized that her unique human qualities would be her competitive advantage.

One of the skills Maya honed was creativity. AI could generate ideas based on existing patterns, but it struggled with true innovation and originality. Maya realized that by nurturing her creative thinking, she could come up with unique solutions, design captivating experiences, and bring a fresh perspective to any project.

Another skill Maya focused on was empathy. AI could analyze sentiments in text or recognize facial expressions, but it couldn't truly understand human emotions. Maya knew that by empathizing with others, she could connect on a deeper level, build meaningful relationships, and deliver products and services that truly resonated with people's needs.

Maya's journey also led her to develop her critical thinking and problem-solving skills. While AI could provide insights and recommendations, it relied on humans to make informed decisions. Maya embraced the role of a critical thinker, analyzing information, evaluating options, and making sound judgments based on context and ethical considerations.

As Maya embarked on her quest to unleash her potential, she discovered a world of endless opportunities. She realized that by embracing lifelong learning, collaborating with AI as a co-creator, and cultivating skills that complemented AI, she could shape a future-proof career and make a lasting impact in the age of AI.

In the next chapter, we will explore how you, like Maya, can master AI tools and technologies to amplify your capabilities and achieve remarkable results. Get ready to dive into the world of AI-driven possibilities and unlock your true potential.

Remember, the age of AI is not a challenge to be

feared but an extraordinary invitation to explore new frontiers. Embrace it, and let your potential soar.

CHAPTER 3: NAVIGATING THE CHANGING LANDSCAPE OF WORK

In the bustling city of New York, where skyscrapers touched the clouds and innovation thrived, lived a young man named David. He had always been passionate about his career and dedicated himself to honing his skills in the field of finance. But as the age of artificial intelligence dawned upon the world, David, like many others, couldn't help but feel a tinge of anxiety about the changing landscape of work.

The news headlines were filled with stories of AI advancements and automation, creating a wave of uncertainty and fear among workers. People wondered, "Will AI replace us? Will our jobs become obsolete?" David, too, found himself grappling with these concerns, questioning the future of his profession.

To gain a deeper understanding of the situation, David began exploring the experiences of individuals who had faced similar uncertainties in the past. He came across the story of the Industrial Revolution, where machines took over manual labor, causing upheaval and displacement for many workers. Yet, as time went on, new industries emerged, and workers adapted by acquiring new skills and finding new avenues for growth.

This historical perspective provided David with a glimmer of hope. He realized that while AI might disrupt certain job roles, it also had the potential to create new opportunities and reshape the nature of work. Armed with this knowledge, he set out to navigate the changing landscape of work, ready to embrace the challenges and seek out the possibilities that lay ahead.

Adaptability: The Key to Thriving in the AI Era

David understood that in the age of AI, adaptability

was crucial. He recognized that the skills he had developed in finance might need to evolve to align with the changing needs of the industry. So, he began his journey of upskilling and reskilling, seeking out new knowledge and acquiring expertise in emerging areas that complemented AI technologies.

One of the skills David focused on was data analysis. He understood that AI excelled at processing vast amounts of data, but it needed human insight to derive meaningful conclusions. By becoming proficient in data analytics, David could leverage AI as a powerful tool in his decision-making process, extracting valuable insights to drive strategic financial planning.

Additionally, David recognized the importance of cultivating a growth mindset. He embraced the idea that learning was a lifelong journey, and the AI era presented ample opportunities for continuous growth. By staying curious, being open to new ideas, and adapting to change, he could position himself as a valuable asset in the evolving world of work.

The Rise of Hybrid Roles: Blending Human Expertise with AI

As David delved deeper into his research, he discovered a new trend in the job market—the rise of hybrid roles. These positions combined the unique strengths of humans with the capabilities of AI, creating a powerful synergy that allowed for unprecedented productivity and innovation.

For example, he learned about Sarah, a customer service representative who had transformed her role by working alongside AI-powered chatbots. By collaborating with these virtual assistants, Sarah could handle routine inquiries more efficiently, freeing up time to focus on complex customer issues that required a human touch. The chatbots acted as her partners, gathering data, analyzing customer sentiment, and providing real-time suggestions, enhancing the overall customer experience.

David also encountered the story of Alex, a marketing professional who leveraged AI-driven analytics to optimize advertising campaigns. By utilizing AI algorithms, Alex could identify target demographics, tailor messages to specific audiences, and track campaign performance in real time. The marriage of human creativity and AI-driven insights allowed him to deliver more impactful and personalized marketing strategies.

These examples inspired David, showing him that the changing landscape of work didn't necessarily mean replacement but rather a transformation of roles and responsibilities. He realized that by embracing AI as a collaborative partner, he could unlock new levels of productivity and effectiveness in his own profession.

Resilience: Thriving in Uncertain Times

The journey of navigating the changing landscape of work was not without its challenges. David encountered setbacks and faced moments of doubt along the way. But he understood that resilience was the key to weathering these storms and emerging stronger.

David sought out support networks and communities of professionals who were also navigating the AI era. He engaged in discussions, shared experiences, and learned from their journeys. Together, they discovered innovative ways to integrate AI technologies into their work while preserving the core values of their respective professions.

Furthermore, David discovered the importance of maintaining a healthy work-life balance. As technology advanced and work became increasingly interconnected, it was crucial to set boundaries and prioritize self-care. By nurturing his physical and mental well-being, David could bring his best self to the professional arena and adapt more effectively to the changing demands of the AI era.

Embracing the Future of Work

As David continued his journey of navigating the changing landscape of work, he realized that the fears he once harbored about AI replacing humans were misplaced. The age of AI was not a threat but an invitation—an invitation to embrace new opportunities, acquire new skills, and redefine the future of work.

Through adaptability, the rise of hybrid roles, and resilience in the face of uncertainty, David discovered his path to success in the AI era. He learned to harness the power of AI as a collaborative partner and leverage his unique human qualities to make a lasting impact.

The changing landscape of work was not an obstacle to be overcome but a canvas on which David and countless others could paint their futures. The age of AI had arrived, and with it came endless possibilities for those who dared to embrace it.

In the second part of this book, we will explore how you can collaborate with AI as your powerful ally and master the tools and technologies that will amplify your capabilities in the age of AI. Get ready to unlock your full potential and embark on a transformative journey of growth and success.

PART II: AI WITH YOU

"Artificial intelligence will be a boon to humanity, enhancing our capabilities and enabling us to solve complex problems with greater efficiency."

CHAPTER 4: COLLABORATING WITH AI—YOUR POWERFUL ALLIES

Please meet a young woman named Emily. She is an ambitious marketer who had always strived for excellence in her field. With the rise of artificial intelligence, Emily knew that she needed to forge a new path—a path that involved collaborating with AI as her powerful ally.

Emily had heard stories of AI replacing jobs and feared that her role as a marketer might be at risk. However, she realized that embracing AI could be the key to unlocking her full potential and staying ahead in the rapidly evolving world of work. Now, I want to introduce you to Emily's strategic plan for staying successful in the AI era.

Step 1: Understanding the Role of AI

Emily embarked on a journey to demystify AI and understand how it could enhance her capabilities as a marketer. She discovered that AI had the power to process vast amounts of data, extract meaningful insights, and automate repetitive tasks. Armed with this knowledge, she saw AI not as a rival but as a valuable tool that could amplify her creativity, improve decision-making, and provide a competitive edge.

Action Step: To stay ahead, familiarize yourself with the AI technologies relevant to your field. Understand their capabilities and explore how they can complement your skills and expertise.

Step 2: Augmenting Creativity with AI

One of the most exciting aspects of collaborating with AI was the opportunity to augment creativity. Emily learned about AI-powered tools that could generate ideas, analyze trends, and even create content. These tools acted as her partners, freeing up her time to focus on more strategic and innovative initiatives.

For instance, Emily explored AI-driven image recognition technology that could identify visual trends in social media posts. By leveraging this tool, she gained valuable insights into her target audience's preferences, allowing her to craft visually appealing and impactful marketing campaigns.

Action Step: Identify AI-powered tools that can enhance your creative processes. Experiment with them, and embrace the fresh perspectives they bring. Combine your human creativity with AI insights to create compelling and engaging content.

Step 3: Enhancing Decision-making with AI Insights

In the age of AI, data reigned supreme. Emily understood that AI could analyze vast amounts of data, uncover patterns, and provide actionable insights. She sought out AI-powered analytics platforms that could help her make data-driven decisions and optimize her marketing strategies.

Emily discovered a platform that utilized machine learning algorithms to analyze customer behavior and preferences. By leveraging this tool, she gained a deeper understanding of her audience, allowing her to tailor her marketing efforts and deliver personalized experiences. The AI insights empowered her to make informed decisions that yielded tangible results.

Action Step: Explore AI-driven analytics platforms that align with your profession. Harness the power of data to inform your decision-making and drive business outcomes. Don't solely rely on AI, but let it guide you towards smarter choices.

Step 4: Collaborating with AI-Powered Assistants

Emily learned that AI assistants were invaluable allies in her quest for productivity and efficiency. These virtual companions could handle routine tasks, manage schedules, and even assist in research, saving her precious time and energy.

She employed a conversational AI assistant that

could schedule meetings, set reminders, and provide instant answers to frequently asked questions. With this AI-powered assistant by her side, Emily found herself more organized, focused, and able to allocate her time to high-value tasks.

Action Step: Explore AI-powered virtual assistants or chatbots that can help streamline your workflow. Delegate repetitive tasks to them and free up your time for strategic initiatives. Remember to provide proper training and guidance to ensure optimal performance.

Step 5: Ethics and Responsibility in AI Collaboration

As Emily delved deeper into the world of AI collaboration, she recognized the importance of ethics and responsibility. She understood that while AI could be a powerful ally, it was essential to ensure its ethical use and mitigate potential biases.

Emily took the initiative to stay informed about AI ethics and best practices. She actively participated in discussions and engaged with experts to understand the ethical implications of AI in her profession. By doing so, she ensured that her AI collaborations aligned with her values and contributed positively to society.

Action Step: Stay informed about AI ethics and participate in discussions surrounding responsible AI use. Consider the ethical implications of AI in your work and strive to use AI in ways that align with your values and benefit all stakeholders.

Your AI-Powered Future Awaits

Through her journey of collaborating with AI, Emily discovered that AI was not a threat but a powerful ally. By embracing AI, she unlocked new levels of creativity, made data-driven decisions, and increased her productivity. AI became an indispensable partner in her professional journey.

To stay ahead in the AI era, it is essential to view AI as a tool that complements and amplifies your human capabilities. Augment your creativity, enhance decision-making, and embrace AI-powered assistants. It is here to support you, not to replace you. However, always remember the importance of ethics and responsibility in AI collaboration.

As you embark on your own journey of collaborating with AI, explore the AI technologies relevant to your field, experiment with AI-powered tools, and stay informed about AI ethics. Embrace the opportunities that AI presents and leverage its power to shape a successful and fulfilling career in the age of AI.

CHAPTER 5: MASTERING AI TOOLS AND TECHNOLOGIES

Once you have embraced the AI era and understood its potential, it's time to dive deeper into the world of AI tools and technologies. In this chapter, we will explore how you can master these tools and leverage them to your advantage, propelling your career forward in the age of AI.

Unleashing the Power of AI Tools

Imagine you are a marketing professional seeking to optimize your advertising campaigns. In the past, you relied on intuition and experience to make decisions. But now, with AI tools at your disposal, you can uncover valuable insights and make data-driven decisions with precision.

One such tool is machine learning algorithms, which can analyze vast amounts of data to identify patterns and trends. By utilizing these algorithms, you can create personalized marketing campaigns tailored to individual customer preferences, increasing engagement and conversion rates.

Additionally, natural language processing (NLP) tools enable you to extract valuable information from unstructured text data, such as social media posts or customer reviews. These tools can help you understand customer sentiment, identify emerging trends, and improve your brand's reputation by promptly addressing any concerns or issues raised by customers.

Strategic Plan for Mastering AI Tools and Technologies:

1. Stay Updated: Keep yourself updated with the latest AI tools and technologies by following reputable sources, attending industry conferences, and participating in online courses and workshops.

2. Hands-on Experience: Gain practical experience by working on AI projects or collaborating with AI teams. This hands-on experience will deepen your understanding and enhance your skill set.

3. Experiment and Learn: Take the initiative to experiment with different AI tools and technologies (there are a lot of them available for free). Set up small projects or proof-of-concepts to explore their capabilities and discover how they can be applied in your specific domain.

4. Network and Collaborate: Connect with professionals in the AI field and join communities or forums where you can exchange knowledge and learn from their experiences. Collaboration with experts and enthusiasts can open up new opportunities for growth and learning.

Real-World Examples of Implementing AI in Professional Industries

Now let's explore a few real-world examples of professionals who have successfully mastered AI tools and technologies to thrive in their respective industries:

1. Healthcare: In the field of healthcare, AI tools like computer vision and deep learning algorithms are being used to analyze medical images and diagnose diseases accurately. Radiologists are now leveraging these tools to expedite the diagnosis process and provide more precise treatment recommendations.

2. Finance: Financial institutions are utilizing AI tools for fraud detection and prevention. Machine learning algorithms can analyze vast amounts of financial transaction data in real-time, identifying suspicious patterns and alerting authorities to potentially fraudulent activities.

3. Manufacturing: AI-powered predictive maintenance tools are revolutionizing the manufacturing industry. By analyzing sensor data from machinery and equipment, these tools can predict maintenance needs, allowing companies to schedule repairs and prevent costly breakdowns.

Action Plan for Mastering AI Tools and Technologies to Thrive in Your Industry:

1. Identify Relevant Tools: Research and identify AI tools and technologies that are relevant to your industry and job role. Consider factors such as ease of use, compatibility with existing systems, and potential impact on your work processes.

2. Obtain Training and Certification: Seek out training programs or courses that specialize in the specific AI tools and technologies you wish to master. Many online platforms offer certifications that validate your skills and enhance your credibility.

3. Apply Tools in Real Projects: Look for opportunities to apply the tools and technologies you have learned in real-world projects. This practical experience will solidify your understanding and showcase your ability to leverage AI for tangible results.

4. Continual Learning: Keep learning and adapting as AI technologies evolve. Stay updated with the latest advancements, research papers, and industry trends to maintain your expertise and remain at the forefront of AI innovation.

By mastering AI tools and technologies, you equip yourself with a powerful arsenal to tackle complex challenges and seize opportunities in the AI era. The key lies in continuous learning, practical application, and a willingness to adapt to the evolving landscape of AI.

Remember, the goal is not to replace human intelligence but to augment it. Embrace these tools as your allies and leverage their capabilities to achieve remarkable outcomes in your professional journey. The AI era holds immense potential, and by mastering the tools of this era, you can stay at the forefront of innovation and secure a successful future.

Keep reading to discover how you can develop the skills of the future in Chapter 6.

CHAPTER 6: DEVELOPING THE SKILLS OF THE FUTURE

Once upon a time, in a quaint little town called Norcross, lived two friends, Alex and Bella. They were both talented individuals with big dreams and aspirations. They had witnessed the incredible advancements brought about by Artificial Intelligence (AI) in their town and the world beyond. But they had different perspectives on the matter.

Alex was wary of AI, fearing that it might replace human jobs and render traditional skills obsolete. Bella, on the other hand, saw AI as an opportunity to enhance her existing skills and develop new ones, believing that it could be a powerful ally rather than a threat.

One day, the town hosted an AI Expo, where experts showcased the latest AI technologies and their applications across various industries. Excited and curious, Alex and Bella attended the event together.

As they wandered through the booths, they saw AI-powered machines and algorithms demonstrating their capabilities. Alex's anxiety grew with each display, while Bella's eyes sparkled with enthusiasm.

"I'm afraid AI will take over everything! What will happen to our jobs and the skills we've honed all these years?" Alex worriedly questioned.

Bella smiled reassuringly. "I understand your concerns but look around. AI is here to stay, and we have two options: resist or adapt. I choose to embrace it and develop the skills that will keep me relevant and valuable in this AI era."

Alex pondered her words as they continued exploring the Expo. They came across a presentation about AI and Human Collaboration.

"Collaboration between AI and humans is the way forward," the speaker emphasized. "AI excels at processing vast amounts of data and automating repetitive tasks, while humans possess creativity, emotional intelligence, and critical thinking skills."

The presentation struck a chord with Bella, reinforcing her belief in the potential for humans and AI to complement each other.

Action Plan 1: Embrace AI-Human Collaboration

1. Be Open-Minded: Accept that AI is changing the landscape of work and acknowledge the benefits of collaborating with AI tools in your industry.

2. Identify Opportunities: Explore areas where AI can enhance your abilities and efficiency, making you more valuable in your professional field.

3. Emphasize Human Skills: Focus on developing uniquely human skills like creativity, problem-solving, empathy, and adaptability, which are irreplaceable by AI.

4. Stay Curious: Continuously learn about the latest AI advancements and how they can be applied in your industry.

5. Seek Feedback: Ask for feedback from colleagues and supervisors on how AI tools can optimize your workflow and identify areas for improvement.

As the day went on, they attended workshops on AI-driven technologies like Natural Language Processing (NLP) and Computer Vision. They watched demonstrations of how NLP algorithms analyzed vast amounts of text data, while computer vision systems accurately identified objects and patterns in images and videos.

Alex was fascinated by the possibilities but also felt overwhelmed. "How can I ever learn to use these complex AI tools?" he wondered.

Bella, sensing his apprehension, said, "Learning new skills takes time and effort, but it's achievable. Let's start small and gradually build our knowledge."

Action Plan 2: Master AI Tools and Technologies from Scratch

1. Start with Basics: Begin with introductory courses on AI and machine learning to understand the fundamental concepts.

2. Choose Relevance: Focus on AI tools that align with your industry and job role.

3. Online Courses: Enroll in online platforms offering AI courses, such as LinkedIn Learning, Coursera, edX, or Udacity, which provide flexibility and self-paced learning.

4. AI Communities: Join AI communities and forums where you can interact with experts and enthusiasts, gaining insights and support.

5. Hands-On Projects: Undertake practical projects that involve AI tools and technologies, applying your newfound knowledge in real-world scenarios.

Throughout the Expo, Alex witnessed various success stories of individuals who had embraced AI and thrived in their respective fields.

One such story that caught his attention was about a marketer named Emily (whom we met in the previous chapter). She had developed expertise in using AI-powered marketing tools, enabling her to create stunning ads more efficiently. Rather than fearing automation, Emily embraced it and leveraged AI to enhance her creative process.

Inspired by these stories and Bella's encouragement, Alex realized that developing the skills of the future was within his reach. He understood that the key was not to resist or compete with AI but to adapt, learn, and collaborate.

As they left the Expo, Alex looked at Bella and said, "You were right all along. The AI era presents challenges, but it also offers incredible opportunities for growth and success. Let's embark on this journey together, supporting each other along the way."

Bella smiled, knowing that with the right mindset, continuous learning, and a willingness to adapt, they could navigate the changing landscape of work and thrive in the AI era.

By embracing AI-human collaboration, mastering AI tools and technologies, and continuously developing their skills, Alex and Bella embarked on a path that would unlock their potential and ensure their success in the ever-evolving world shaped by Artificial Intelligence.

As you, the reader, embark on your own journey, remember that the power lies in your hands. Embrace the AI era, learn, adapt, and forge ahead with confidence, knowing that the skills you develop today will shape your future in the age of AI.

PART III: AI FOR YOU

"Artificial intelligence is not a threat, but an opportunity to redefine the boundaries of human potential and create a better future for all."

CHAPTER 7: EXPLORING AI-DRIVEN INDUSTRIES AND OPPORTUNITIES

In a world on the cusp of an AI revolution, individuals who were curious and forward-thinking saw an opportunity to embrace the power of artificial intelligence. They recognized that AI had the potential to transform industries, create new possibilities, and open doors to exciting career opportunities. These individuals understood that to thrive in the AI era, they needed to explore AI-driven industries and seize emerging opportunities.

In this chapter, we will embark on a journey of discovery, where we will delve into the realms of AI-driven industries and uncover the vast array of opportunities that await us. We will explore how AI is reshaping various sectors, from healthcare to finance, from transportation to marketing, and beyond. By understanding the potential applications of AI in different fields, we can position ourselves for success and find our niche in the ever-evolving landscape.

The Power of AI in Healthcare

Let's start our exploration by diving into the realm of healthcare, a field that is being revolutionized by advancements in AI. Imagine a world where medical diagnoses are more accurate, treatment plans are personalized, and patient outcomes are improved— all thanks to the power of AI in cooperation with humans.

AI-driven technologies such as machine learning algorithms and computer vision are enabling healthcare professionals to analyze vast amounts of medical data, identify patterns, and make data-driven decisions. For example, AI algorithms can assist radiologists in detecting early signs of diseases in medical imaging, helping to improve diagnostic accuracy and speed up the detection process. Furthermore, AI-powered chatbots are being deployed to provide instant medical advice, enhancing access to healthcare services and empowering individuals to make informed decisions about their well-being.

To explore opportunities in the healthcare industry, consider the following action plan:

1. Stay Informed: Keep abreast of the latest developments in AI applications in healthcare by following reputable sources, attending conferences, and joining professional networks.

2. Gain Domain Knowledge: Acquire a solid understanding of healthcare processes, regulations, and challenges. Consider pursuing specialized courses or certifications to enhance your expertise.

3. Collaborate with Healthcare Professionals: Seek opportunities to collaborate with healthcare practitioners, researchers, and organizations to gain practical insights and contribute to AI-driven healthcare solutions.

4. Develop Ethical AI Skills: Understand the ethical implications of AI in healthcare and familiarize yourself with relevant guidelines and regulations. Aim to promote responsible and ethical AI practices within the industry.

Transforming Finance with AI

Now, let's shift our focus to the finance industry, which is undergoing a significant transformation driven by AI. From fraud detection to algorithmic trading, AI is revolutionizing the way financial institutions operate and make decisions.

AI algorithms can analyze vast financial datasets, detect anomalies, and identify patterns that human analysts may overlook. This helps financial institutions in areas such as risk assessment, fraud detection, and portfolio optimization. Additionally, AI-powered chatbots and virtual assistants are being employed to enhance customer experiences, providing personalized recommendations and streamlined financial services.

To explore opportunities in the finance industry, consider the following action plan:

1. Enhance Financial Acumen: Develop a strong understanding of financial concepts, markets, and industry trends. Consider pursuing relevant certifications, such as financial analysis or risk management, to bolster your expertise.

2. Deepen Technical Skills: Acquire proficiency in data analysis, machine learning, and programming languages commonly used in the finance industry, such as Python or R. This will enable you to effectively leverage AI tools and technologies.

3. Network and Collaborate: Engage with professionals in the finance industry through networking events, online communities, and industry-specific conferences. Seek opportunities to collaborate on AI projects or join interdisciplinary teams.

4. Stay Agile and Adaptive: As the finance industry evolves rapidly, embrace a mindset of continuous learning and adaptability. Keep up with emerging trends and technologies to remain at the forefront of the industry.

Unleashing AI's Potential in Marketing

Marketing is another domain where AI is making a

significant impact. AI-driven tools and techniques are enabling marketers to gain deeper insights into consumer behavior, personalize marketing campaigns, and optimize customer experiences.

AI-powered analytics platforms can process vast amounts of data, uncover hidden patterns, and predict consumer preferences, allowing marketers to tailor their strategies accordingly. Chatbots and virtual assistants are also being employed to engage with customers, providing personalized recommendations and delivering seamless experiences across various digital channels.

To explore opportunities in the marketing industry, consider the following action plan:

1. Develop Data Analytics Skills: Familiarize yourself with data analysis techniques, including data mining, predictive modeling, and customer segmentation. Acquire proficiency in analytics tools such as Google Analytics or marketing automation platforms.

2. Deepen Understanding of Consumer Behavior: Study consumer psychology, market research methodologies, and digital marketing trends. Stay informed about emerging technologies and their impact on consumer behavior.

3. Embrace Creative and Strategic Thinking: Combine your knowledge of AI with creative thinking to devise innovative marketing strategies. Explore how AI can enhance personalization, automate repetitive tasks, and optimize marketing campaigns.

4. Build a Strong Digital Presence: Demonstrate your expertise by creating a personal brand through online platforms, such as blogs, social media, and professional networks. Share valuable insights and engage with industry professionals to expand your network.

By actively exploring AI-driven industries, understanding their potential, and taking concrete steps toward developing the necessary skills, you can position yourself for success in the AI era. Remember, it is not enough to simply observe from the sidelines. You must actively engage and seize the opportunities that arise.

Your Personal Action Plan to Stay in Demand in the AI Era:

1. Stay Informed: Regularly read industry publications, attend conferences, and follow thought leaders in AI-driven industries to stay up-to-date with the latest trends and opportunities.

2. Identify Industry Alignment: Assess your skills, interests, and values to identify AI-driven industries that align with your passions and goals.

3. Continuous Learning: Invest time in learning about the specific applications and use cases of AI in your chosen industry. Seek out online courses, workshops, or mentorship programs to deepen your knowledge.

4. Networking and Collaboration: Engage with professionals and organizations in AI-driven industries through networking events, online communities, and industry-specific platforms. Collaborate on projects and seek mentorship opportunities to gain practical experience.

5. Gain Practical Experience: Look for internships, apprenticeships, or volunteer opportunities in AI-driven industries to gain hands-on experience and enhance your understanding of industry dynamics.

6. Adaptability and Resilience: Embrace a mindset of adaptability and resilience, as AI-driven industries continue to evolve. Be open to new challenges and opportunities that may arise and continually update your skills to stay relevant.

By following this action plan and staying proactive in exploring AI-driven industries, you can position yourself for a successful and fulfilling career in the AI era. Exciting opportunities await those who embrace the potential of AI and take action to shape their own future.

As we conclude this chapter, remember that exploring AI-driven industries and opportunities requires an open mind, a thirst for knowledge, and a willingness to adapt. The AI revolution is here, and it is reshaping the world as we know it. By embracing the power of AI, developing relevant skills, and actively seeking out opportunities, you can position yourself at the forefront of this transformative era. Stay curious, stay dedicated, and unlock the boundless potential that awaits you in the AI-driven future.

In the next chapter, we will delve into the importance of building a personal brand in the AI age.

CHAPTER 8: BUILDING A PERSONAL BRAND IN THE AI AGE

In this chapter, we will delve into the importance of building a personal brand in the AI era. We will explore how effectively showcasing your skills, knowledge, and unique value proposition can create exciting opportunities and help you stand out in a competitive landscape.

The Rise of Personal Branding in the AI Age

In the age of AI, where technological advancements and automation are reshaping industries, the concept of personal branding has become more crucial than ever. As AI continues to evolve and transform the workforce, individuals must proactively position themselves as valuable assets in the digital landscape. Building a personal brand allows you to showcase your unique skills, expertise, and qualities that set you apart from the crowd.

Addressing the Fears: AI Replacing People

Before we delve into the strategies for building a personal brand in the AI age, let's address once more one of the most common fears associated with AI: the fear of machines replacing human workers. It is natural to have concerns about job security and the impact of automation on employment opportunities. However, it is important to recognize that AI is not a threat but a tool that can enhance our capabilities and create new opportunities.

History has shown us that technological advancements often lead to the creation of new jobs and industries. While certain routine and repetitive tasks may be automated, AI also generates a demand for individuals who can harness its power, develop innovative solutions, and leverage its potential. By building a strong personal brand, you can position yourself as an indispensable contributor in the AI era.

Understanding Personal Branding in the AI Age

Personal branding is the intentional process of establishing and promoting your unique identity, expertise, and value proposition in the digital landscape. It involves crafting a compelling narrative that highlights your skills, knowledge, and achievements while building a strong online presence and network.

In the AI age, personal branding takes on a new level of importance. It allows you to demonstrate your adaptability, creativity, and ability to collaborate with AI technologies. It showcases your ability to leverage AI tools, understands their limitations, and apply them strategically to solve complex problems. A well-developed personal brand in the AI age can open doors to exciting opportunities, collaborations, and recognition in your industry.

Crafting Your Personal Brand in the AI Age

1. Define Your Unique Value Proposition

To build a strong personal brand in the AI age, you must first identify your unique value proposition. Reflect on your skills, strengths, and experiences that differentiate you from others. Consider the specific areas where AI intersects with your expertise and how you can leverage it to create value. Are you a data scientist with a deep understanding of AI algorithms? Are you a marketer with a knack for leveraging AI-driven analytics to drive results? Define your niche and highlight what makes you stand out.

Real-World Example: Meet Sarah, a digital marketer with a passion for AI-driven analytics. She has developed a deep understanding of marketing automation tools and data analytics platforms. Sarah identifies her unique value proposition as the ability to harness the power of AI to optimize marketing campaigns, drive personalized customer experiences, and uncover actionable insights for her clients.

Action Plan:

- Conduct a self-assessment to identify your unique skills, experiences, and expertise.

- Research the intersection between your field and AI

to discover how you can leverage AI to enhance your value proposition.

- Refine your personal brand statement that captures your unique value proposition and communicates it effectively to your target audience.

2. Establish a Strong Online Presence

In the digital age, building an online presence is vital for personal branding. Establishing a strong online presence enables you to reach a wider audience, showcase your expertise, and engage with industry professionals.

Real-World Example: Jack, a software developer specializing in AI applications, maintains a professional website where he regularly publishes articles and shares his insights on AI-related topics. He also actively participates in online communities and industry forums, demonstrating his expertise and building relationships with fellow professionals.

Action Plan:

- Create a professional website or portfolio that showcases your expertise, achievements, and thought leadership in AI.

- Optimize your social media profiles to reflect your personal brand and engage with relevant communities and professionals in your industry.

- Consistently share valuable content, such as articles, case studies, or videos, that demonstrate your knowledge and expertise in AI.

3. Cultivate a Network of AI Professionals

In the AI age, collaboration and networking are key to staying relevant and expanding your opportunities. Building relationships with AI professionals thought leaders, and experts can provide valuable insights, mentorship, and potential collaborations.

Real-World Example: Emma, a data scientist specializing in AI-driven healthcare solutions, actively participates in AI-focused meetups, conferences, and industry events. By attending these events and engaging in discussions with experts in her field, Emma expands her network and stays updated on the latest trends and advancements in AI.

Action Plan:

- Attend industry conferences, webinars, and meetups focused on AI to connect with professionals in your field.

- Engage in online communities and forums related to AI to share knowledge, ask questions, and build relationships.

- Seek mentorship opportunities from experienced AI professionals who can guide you on your career journey.

4. Continuous Learning and Adaptability

To thrive in the AI age, continuous learning and adaptability are essential. AI technologies are rapidly evolving, and staying updated with the latest trends, tools, and methodologies is crucial for maintaining a competitive edge.

Real-World Example: Mark, a business consultant, dedicates time each week to learning about emerging AI technologies and their applications in various industries. He takes online courses, reads industry publications, and engages in hands-on projects to develop practical skills in AI.

Action Plan:

- Identify learning resources such as online courses, tutorials, and books that can help you deepen your knowledge of AI.

- Allocate regular time for learning and experimentation with AI tools and technologies.

- Stay updated on industry news and advancements through reputable sources and subscribe to AI-related newsletters or publications.

Thriving in the AI Age with Your Personal Brand

In the rapidly evolving landscape of the AI age, building a personal brand is no longer a choice but a necessity. By embracing personal branding, you position yourself as a valuable asset in the AI-driven industries and create opportunities for career growth, collaborations, and recognition.

Remember, AI is not here to replace us but to augment our abilities. By leveraging AI tools, developing your skills, and building a strong personal brand, you can thrive in the AI age and become a driving force of innovation and success in your industry. Embrace the power of personal branding in the AI age, and embark on a journey of limitless possibilities.

Your Personal Action Plan for Today:

- Reflect on the strategies outlined in this chapter and develop a personalized action plan to build your personal brand in the AI age.

- Set goals and timelines for implementing each step of the action plan.

- Regularly review and adapt your action plan to stay aligned with the evolving AI landscape.

Remember, building a personal brand is a continuous process. It requires consistency, perseverance, and a commitment to lifelong learning. Embrace the opportunities that AI presents, and seize the chance to position yourself as a leader and innovator in your industry.

The AI age is yours to conquer, and your personal brand will be your guiding light in this transformative era.

CHAPTER 9: CREATING YOUR FUTURE-PROOF CAREER ROADMAP

As we stand at the cusp of the AI revolution, the need for a future-proof career has never been more evident. The rapid advancements in artificial intelligence and automation are reshaping industries and the job market, prompting individuals to take charge of their career paths like never before.

The Journey Towards a Future-Proof Career

In this chapter, we embark on a journey of self-discovery and strategic planning to create a future-proof career roadmap that will navigate the waves of change and lead us toward success in the AI age.

The Tale of Lucy Who Embraced Change and the Pursuit of a Future-Proof Career

Meet Lucy, a skilled graphic designer who has been working in the creative industry for over a decade. She has always been passionate about her craft, blending her artistic talent with cutting-edge design software to create captivating visuals. However, as she witnesses the rise of AI-powered design tools, Lucy begins to feel a sense of uncertainty about her future in the field. The fear of her job being automated fills her with apprehension and doubt.

One day, during an industry conference, Lucy encounters a keynote speaker who shares an inspiring tale of career transformation in the face of AI disruption. This speaker, Ellie, was once a traditional accountant whose role was largely manual and repetitive. When AI-driven financial analysis tools emerged, Ellie chose to embrace the change rather than resist it. She honed her skills in data analytics, machine learning, and financial modeling, transforming herself into a sought-after financial consultant, working alongside AI to deliver unparalleled insights to her clients.

Ellie's story resonates deeply with Lucy, igniting a spark of curiosity and determination within her. She realizes that the future is not set in stone and that she has the power to shape her destiny in the AI age. With a renewed sense of purpose, Lucy sets out on a quest to create her future-proof career roadmap.

Step 1: Self-Reflection and Skill Assessment

Creating a future-proof career roadmap begins with self-reflection. Take a moment to introspect and assess your skills, strengths, and areas of passion. Identify the uniquely human skills and those that can be augmented by AI technologies.

Action Plan:

- Create a list of your core skills and expertise, both technical and soft skills.

- Research the impact of AI on your industry and identify the skills that will be in high demand in the AI age.

- Seek feedback from colleagues, mentors, or career advisors to gain valuable insights into your strengths and areas for improvement.

Step 2: Embrace Lifelong Learning

In the age of AI, learning is a lifelong pursuit. To future-proof your career, you must adopt a growth mindset and commit to continuous learning. Stay updated with the latest advancements in your field, explore emerging technologies, and seek opportunities to upskill or reskill.

Action Plan:

- Enroll in online courses, workshops, or boot camps to learn new skills relevant to the AI age.

- Attend conferences, webinars, and industry events to gain exposure to cutting-edge technologies and trends.

- Join professional organizations or online communities to network with like-minded individuals and experts in your field.

Step 3: Leverage AI as Your Partner

AI is not your competitor. It can be your most valuable ally. Embrace AI as a tool that can enhance your productivity, creativity, and decision-making. Understand its capabilities and limitations to leverage it effectively in your work.

Action Plan:

- Identify areas in your profession where AI can add value and streamline processes.

- Experiment with AI-driven tools and technologies to experience their potential firsthand.

- Collaborate with AI systems to gain insights and improve the quality of your work.

Step 4: Cultivate a Growth-Oriented Mindset

In a rapidly changing world, adaptability and resilience are key to success. Embrace change, view failures as learning opportunities, and continually seek ways to grow and improve.

Action Plan:

- Embrace new challenges and step out of your comfort zone to develop new skills.

- Learn from setbacks and view them as opportunities to refine your approach.

- Foster a mindset of continuous improvement and

celebrate your achievements along the way.

Step 5: Stay Agile and Open to Opportunities

In the AI age, careers are no longer linear. Embrace agility and be open to new opportunities that may come your way. Keep an eye on industry trends and be proactive in seeking out projects or roles that align with your career goals.

Action Plan:

- Stay connected with industry trends through networking, reading industry publications, and attending relevant events.

- Seek out cross-functional projects or collaborations that allow you to gain exposure to different aspects of your industry.

- Be open to exploring new roles or industries that may offer exciting AI-driven opportunities.

Your Future-Proof Career Awaits

Creating a future-proof career roadmap is a dynamic

process that requires self-reflection, continuous learning, and adaptability. By following the steps outlined in this chapter and taking proactive action, you can navigate the waves of AI disruption and shape a career that thrives in the AI age.

Remember, your career journey is unique, and there is no one-size-fits-all approach. Embrace the power of self-discovery, leverage the potential of AI as your ally, and cultivate a growth-oriented mindset. With determination, resilience, and a strategic roadmap, you can embark on a fulfilling and future-proof career in the AI age.

Your Personal Action Plan for Today:

- Reflect on the strategies outlined in this chapter and develop a personalized action plan for your future-proof career roadmap.

- Set realistic goals and establish timelines for achieving each milestone.

- Regularly evaluate and adjust your roadmap as you progress and as the AI landscape evolves.

The future is yours to shape, and with the right mindset and strategic planning, you can build a career that not only withstands the winds of change but thrives in the AI age. Your future-proof career awaits—let the journey begin!

FINAL THOUGHTS: THE JOURNEY AHEAD

"Artificial intelligence will be part of our future and will make us smarter, but it will not make us wiser."

As we reach the final chapter of this book, it is time to pause and reflect on the incredible journey we have embarked upon. We have traversed the realms of the AI revolution, exploring its promises, challenges, and the remarkable opportunities it presents. From embracing the AI era to developing future-proof skills, from collaborating with AI to exploring AI-driven industries, we have delved into the depths of this transformative landscape. Now, as we stand at the precipice of the future, let us take a moment to contemplate the path we have traveled and the road that lies ahead.

Throughout our exploration, one theme has emerged as a steadfast guiding principle: the symbiotic relationship between humans and AI. We have witnessed firsthand how collaboration between human ingenuity and the power of intelligent technologies can result in extraordinary achievements. It is not a question of humans versus machines, but rather a harmonious partnership where our unique qualities and abilities intertwine with the capabilities of AI to shape a better tomorrow.

In the face of the fears and uncertainties that initially gripped us, we have learned that the true power lies in our adaptability and resilience. Instead of allowing anxiety to cloud our judgment, we have embraced change and seized the opportunities presented by the AI revolution. We have understood that the pursuit of a future-proof career requires continuous learning, upskilling, and an unwavering commitment to personal growth.

Lucy, whose journey we have followed throughout this book, serves as a testament to the transformative power of embracing change. She faced her fears head-on, took bold steps to acquire new skills, and leveraged AI tools and technologies to enhance her work. Her story embodies the potential that lies within each one of us—a potential waiting to be unleashed, nurtured, and channeled toward creating a fulfilling and successful future.

But Lucy's journey is not an isolated tale. It is a microcosm of the larger narrative that is unfolding in the world today. The AI revolution is not confined to a select few. It is a global phenomenon that impacts every industry, every profession, and every individual. As we bid farewell to this book, we must remember that the journey does not end here. It is merely the beginning of a lifelong commitment to growth and adaptability in the face of an ever-evolving technological landscape.

So, what lies ahead on this journey?

The road before us is filled with endless possibilities and exciting new horizons. It is a road that requires us to stay curious, embrace a growth mindset, and continually seek out opportunities for learning and development. The AI revolution is far from reaching its pinnacle. It is an ongoing process of innovation and discovery. As new technologies emerge, as industries transform, and as the very fabric of work evolves, we must be ready to adapt, pivot, and thrive.

To navigate the road ahead, we must equip ourselves with the right mindset and tools. We must be proactive in identifying emerging trends and acquiring the skills necessary to stay ahead of the curve. We must cultivate a deep understanding of ethical considerations surrounding AI and actively participate in shaping its responsible and beneficial implementation.

Additionally, building a strong professional network and personal brand will be paramount in the AI age. By cultivating authentic relationships, showcasing our expertise, and positioning ourselves as thought leaders, we can seize opportunities, open doors, and make a lasting impact in the AI-driven industries we choose to pursue.

As we conclude this book, let yourself carry the lessons we have learned and the insights we have gained. Let yourself embrace the AI revolution as a catalyst for growth and progress, and let yourself harness its power to shape a future that is inclusive, human-centered, and ethically grounded.

Remember, the journey ahead may be filled with challenges, but it is also filled with tremendous potential. It is a journey that invites us to continually evolve, adapt, and push the boundaries of what we thought was possible. With each step we take, with each new skill we acquire, we move closer to unlocking the full potential of the human-

AI partnership and creating a truly transformative world.

So, my fellow adventurer, as we bid farewell, let yourself embark on this journey with renewed vigor and a sense of purpose. Let yourself be fearless in the face of change and seize the opportunities that lie before us. The AI revolution is calling, and the future is ours to shape. Together, we can create a world where the union of human intelligence and artificial intelligence paves the way for a brighter and more prosperous tomorrow.

Safe travels, my friend, and may the path ahead be filled with endless possibilities and remarkable discoveries. The future is now, and it is ours to embrace. Use the strategic plan explained in this book to succeed in the age of artificial intelligence and future-proof your career in the next decades.

THE POWER OF YOUR REVIEW

Your feedback matters! If you found this book valuable, please leave a review on Amazon.

https://www.amazon.com/dp/B0C8ZN1CGK

Your review provides valuable insights for me and helps other readers discover this book.

EXPAND YOUR
AI JOURNEY

If you enjoyed this book, you may also be
interested in exploring other books written
by me. Visit my author page on Amazon:

https://www.amazon.com/author/kuznietsov_ivan

Discover more captivating reads on the intersection
of technology and human potential!

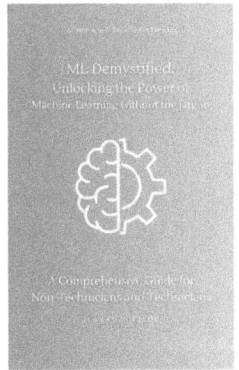
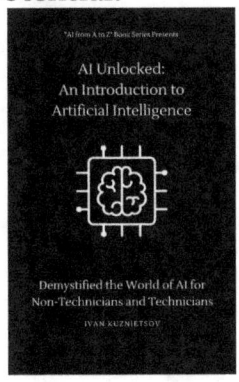

ACKNOWLEDGMENTS

I would like to express my heartfelt gratitude to all those who have contributed to the creation of this book.

To my family and friends, thank you for your unwavering support and encouragement throughout this journey. Your belief in me has been a constant source of inspiration.

I extend my deepest appreciation to the experts and professionals who generously shared their insights and expertise, enriching the content of this book.

To the readers, thank you for your interest and trust in exploring the fascinating world of AI with me. Your curiosity fuels my passion for sharing knowledge.

BIBLIOGRAPHY

1. Brynjolfsson, E., & McAfee, A. (2014). The Second Machine Age: Work, Progress, and Prosperity in a Time of Brilliant Technologies. W. W. Norton & Company.
2. Davenport, T. H., & Kirby, J. (2016). Only Humans Need Apply: Winners and Losers in the Age of Smart Machines. HarperBusiness.
3. Ford, M. (2015). Rise of the Robots: Technology and the Threat of a Jobless Future. Basic Books.
4. Kurzweil, R. (2005). The Singularity Is Near: When Humans Transcend Biology. Penguin Books.
5. McAfee, A., & Brynjolfsson, E. (2017). Machine, Platform, Crowd: Harnessing Our Digital Future. W. W. Norton & Company.
6. O'Neil, C. (2016). Weapons of Math Destruction: How Big Data Increases Inequality and Threatens Democracy. Crown.
7. Russell, S., & Norvig, P. (2016). Artificial

Intelligence: A Modern Approach. Pearson.

8. Smolan, R., & Erwitt, J. (2019). AI: A Visual History. TASCHEN.

9. West, D. M. (2018). The Future of Work: Robots, AI, and Automation. Brookings Institution Press.

www.ingramcontent.com/pod-product-compliance
Lightning Source LLC
Chambersburg PA
CBHW072328290526
45794CB00002B/790